POMPEII

Richard Platt

Illustrated by Manuela Cappon

KINGFISHER

BOSTON

Pompeii

Between the dark shadow of a mountain and the sparkling water of the Bay of Naples, there was once a lively, bustling town. Pompeii was similar to other towns along Italy's western shore. Greeks had settled there, and they were joined by other foreign settlers during the 200s B.C. In later years its citizens included soldiers of the Roman Empire, which ruled the Mediterranean lands of southern Europe.

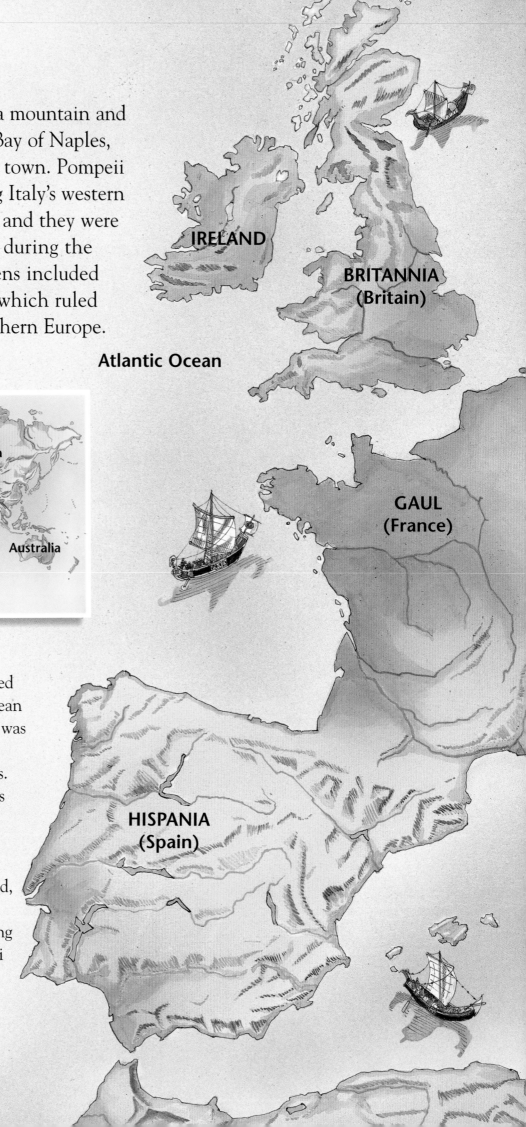

IRELAND

BRITANNIA (Britain)

Atlantic Ocean

Asia

Europe

North America

Africa

South America

Australia

GAUL (France)

Pompeii is on the "shin" of boot-shaped Italy, in the middle of the Mediterranean Sea. Two thousand years ago Pompeii was thriving; its wealthiest citizens owned beautiful, luxuriously decorated homes. Slaves and poorer people worked in its houses, stores, docks, and workshops.

But in A.D. 79 disaster struck. The volcanic mountain, Vesuvius, exploded, and life in Pompeii suddenly ended. Dust and ash fell from the sky, preserving everything that they covered. Pompeii was turned into a perfect, tragic snapshot of Roman life.

HISPANIA (Spain)

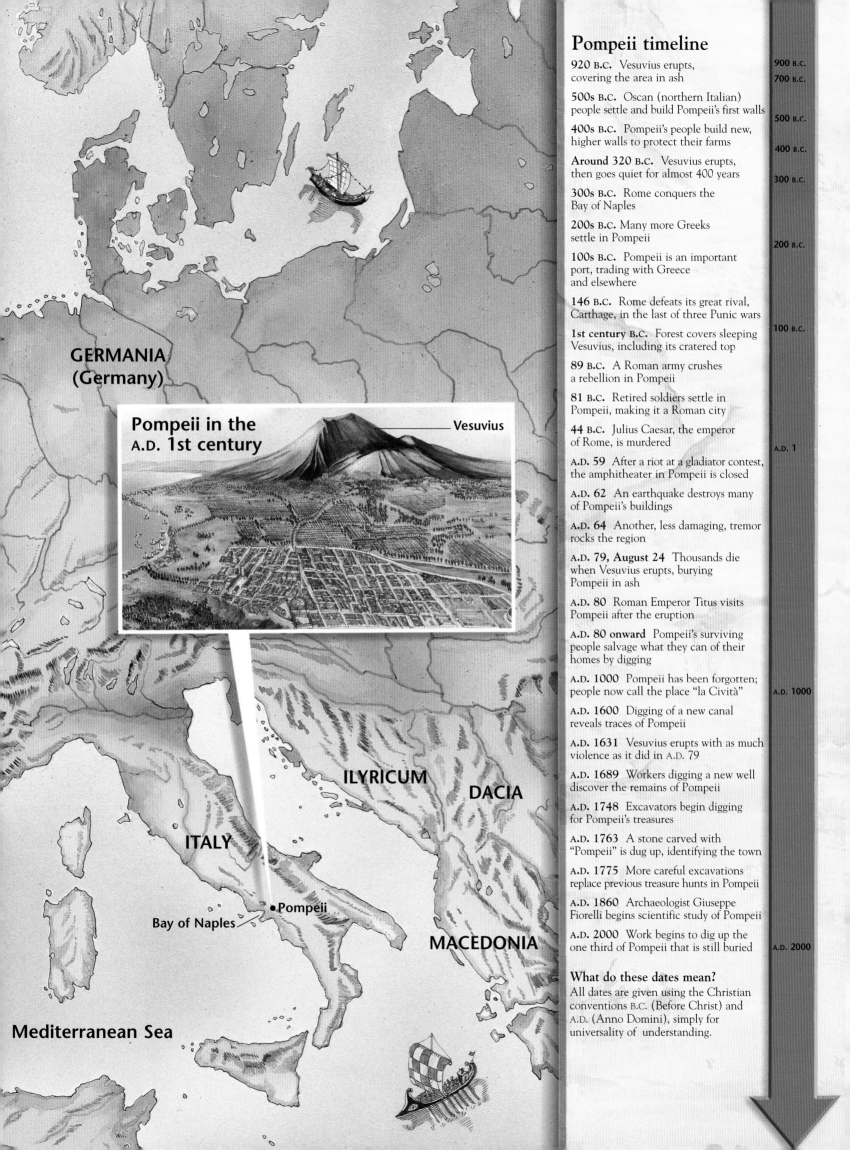

GERMANIA
(Germany)

ITALY

Pompeii

Bay of Naples

Mediterranean Sea

ILYRICUM

DACIA

MACEDONIA

Pompeii in the A.D. 1st century

Vesuvius

Pompeii timeline

920 B.C. Vesuvius erupts, covering the area in ash

500s B.C. Oscan (northern Italian) people settle and build Pompeii's first walls

400s B.C. Pompeii's people build new, higher walls to protect their farms

Around 320 B.C. Vesuvius erupts, then goes quiet for almost 400 years

300s B.C. Rome conquers the Bay of Naples

200s B.C. Many more Greeks settle in Pompeii

100s B.C. Pompeii is an important port, trading with Greece and elsewhere

146 B.C. Rome defeats its great rival, Carthage, in the last of three Punic wars

1st century B.C. Forest covers sleeping Vesuvius, including its cratered top

89 B.C. A Roman army crushes a rebellion in Pompeii

81 B.C. Retired soldiers settle in Pompeii, making it a Roman city

44 B.C. Julius Caesar, the emperor of Rome, is murdered

A.D. 59 After a riot at a gladiator contest, the amphitheater in Pompeii is closed

A.D. 62 An earthquake destroys many of Pompeii's buildings

A.D. 64 Another, less damaging, tremor rocks the region

A.D. 79, August 24 Thousands die when Vesuvius erupts, burying Pompeii in ash

A.D. 80 Roman Emperor Titus visits Pompeii after the eruption

A.D. 80 onward Pompeii's surviving people salvage what they can of their homes by digging

A.D. 1000 Pompeii has been forgotten; people now call the place "la Città"

A.D. 1600 Digging of a new canal reveals traces of Pompeii

A.D. 1631 Vesuvius erupts with as much violence as it did in A.D. 79

A.D. 1689 Workers digging a new well discover the remains of Pompeii

A.D. 1748 Excavators begin digging for Pompeii's treasures

A.D. 1763 A stone carved with "Pompeii" is dug up, identifying the town

A.D. 1775 More careful excavations replace previous treasure hunts in Pompeii

A.D. 1860 Archaeologist Giuseppe Fiorelli begins scientific study of Pompeii

A.D. 2000 Work begins to dig up the one third of Pompeii that is still buried

What do these dates mean?
All dates are given using the Christian conventions B.C. (Before Christ) and A.D. (Anno Domini), simply for universality of understanding.

900 B.C.
700 B.C.
500 B.C.
400 B.C.
300 B.C.
200 B.C.
100 B.C.
A.D. 1
A.D. 1000
A.D. 2000

Contents

The pages that follow trace the history of a typical house in Pompeii. You can see how the house grew as the city flourished. You can watch it crumble in flames and ash with the rest of the city, as it did when Vesuvius erupted. And you can discover how it was found again and restored hundreds of years later.

The city under attack
page 16

Farms and crafts
page 8

The house prospers
page 12

A growing city
page 20

A humble hut
page 6

Inside the atrium
page 14

The town develops
page 10

After the war
page 18

 What does this symbol mean?
This vase shows you where the house is in each busy city scene so that you can follow its story through time.

After the earthquake
page 28

Treasure hunters
page 36

The house at
its peak
page 22

The eruption
page 30

Romantic ruins
page 40

A banquet
page 24

A buried city
page 32

Studying the ruins
page 38

The earthquake
page 26

Forgotten
Pompeii
page 34

A humble hut
750 B.C.

Pompeii begins as not much more than a group of farms, with rough walls enclosing the oldest. Already the town is too big for its boundaries, and some families have started to farm the land nearby. There, beyond the walls, one house stands out. Although it is just a hut, it is in the middle of the most prosperous farm.

The land around the farm supplied almost everything that was needed to build the hut. Solid tree trunks form the frame. The ropes that tie the roof timbers together are made from twisted plant fibers. Stalks from the emmer crop and reeds cut from nearby riverbanks provide the thatched roof. Only the thatcher's metal tools were not made on the farm.

woodland provides timber and foraging areas for pigs

fishing boats moor at the nearby harbor

Grapes are harvested from the vines grown at the foot of Vesuvius and are used for making wine.

a hole at the top of each hut lets out smoke from a cooking fire inside

a boy chases away birds from the emmer crop

the emmer grain is used to make wheat for flour

reapers only cut the heads of stalks to harvest the grain, so the leftover straw can be used for thatching

emmer straw is cut and used for thatching

a shovel made entirely from wood

metal tools are the most valuable of the farmer's possessions

thorn bushes provide natural barbed wire

the fence keeps the pigs in and the wolves out

the volcano has been quiet for more than 100 years

forests cover the lower slopes of Vesuvius

vines are grown at the foot of the slopes

Farmers make offerings to their gods at the temples of the old town, in the southwestern area of Pompeii.

grapevines

this small hut is the beginning of a house that will stand on this site for more than 800 years

the roads in this part of Pompeii are simple tracks

sheep provide milk as well as meat and wool

vegetable plot for growing cabbages, leeks, turnips, and onions

a new thatch is being added to this hut

tame pigs run at the sound of the herder's horn

The farming family works hard; they must do everything by hand. Even the youngest child helps out, scaring away birds and picking bugs off the food plants. If there is enough rain, they will eat well again this year—as long as they can keep the wolves away from the pigs and wild boar out of the grain!

Farms and crafts 380 B.C.

As Pompeii grows and its people thrive, it begins to look less like farmland. Roads and tracks have created a grid of roughly equal-sized plots. In this northern area of Pompeii farmers still grow crops and raise animals within the town walls. But in addition to farming, the town is now home to a new type of work.

a shepherd tends to his flock

cattle graze on the grain spilled at harvest time

wheat has replaced other crops

roofs need replacing when the thatch starts to rot

the hut has grown into a group of farmhouses

splitting logs to make planks for building

squeezing oil from olive pulp

lime render (cement) protects the stone walls of the houses

a donkey turns the olive press

olive pits make good cooking fuel

a fullery (cloth-cleaning house)

track rutted by carts' wheels

wheat produces more grain than the emmer crop that it has replaced

main road

slaves clean fabric in a urine bath

draining the washed fabric

The stone wheels of the press are designed so that they crush the olives but not the pits inside.

8

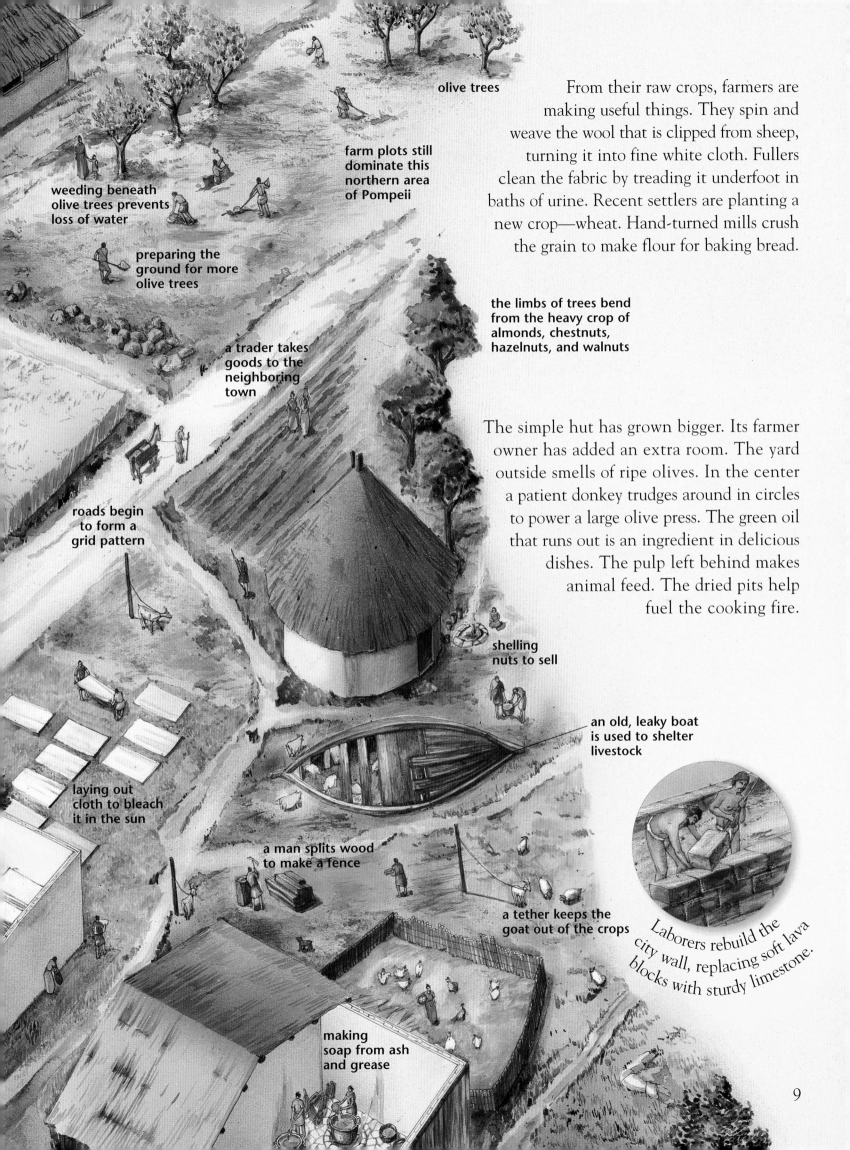

olive trees

farm plots still dominate this northern area of Pompeii

weeding beneath olive trees prevents loss of water

preparing the ground for more olive trees

a trader takes goods to the neighboring town

roads begin to form a grid pattern

the limbs of trees bend from the heavy crop of almonds, chestnuts, hazelnuts, and walnuts

shelling nuts to sell

an old, leaky boat is used to shelter livestock

laying out cloth to bleach it in the sun

a man splits wood to make a fence

a tether keeps the goat out of the crops

making soap from ash and grease

Laborers rebuild the city wall, replacing soft lava blocks with sturdy limestone.

From their raw crops, farmers are making useful things. They spin and weave the wool that is clipped from sheep, turning it into fine white cloth. Fullers clean the fabric by treading it underfoot in baths of urine. Recent settlers are planting a new crop—wheat. Hand-turned mills crush the grain to make flour for baking bread.

The simple hut has grown bigger. Its farmer owner has added an extra room. The yard outside smells of ripe olives. In the center a patient donkey trudges around in circles to power a large olive press. The green oil that runs out is an ingredient in delicious dishes. The pulp left behind makes animal feed. The dried pits help fuel the cooking fire.

The town develops 300 B.C.

Eighty years later Pompeii is flourishing. Where once there were open fields, now there are impressive new houses. The streets echo with foreign voices. Pompeii's harbor, a quarter-mile away, has attracted Greek traders to the town. Their ships bring precious luxuries. On the return voyage, sea captains load up with farm produce and goods that are marked "Made in Pompeii."

Now positioned in the busy heart of the town, the house has again grown in size and status. The farmer owner has bought the plot next door to expand his home. Its walls are smoothly plastered and painted. It is not just farming that has paid for these improvements, buying and selling crops and crafts has also made him rich.

Although it is now a bustling harbor town, Pompeii still has a country feel to it. Ducks waddle through the streets. Flocks of sheep hold up the traffic. And in the busy marketplace Pompeii's newly wealthy merchants make fun of the ragged farmers with their country accents.

The best houses now have roofs covered in red tiles instead of thatch.

tiled roofs

the house is now one of the largest in the local area

wood turner

adding new rooms to the house

main road

store selling luxury fabrics imported from Egypt, in Africa, and from Phoenicia and Syria, to the east of the Mediterranean lands

a trader displays expensive silks from Asia

wealthy Pompeiians buy expensive statues from abroad

sheep graze where grain used to grow

Local crafts include basket weaving.

weaving fabric from wool

deep water well

farms, factories, and houses are closely packed together

blacksmith's workshop

carpenter's store

outdoor fire for casting (molding) metal

copper worker uses metal brought from foreign mines

tools and weapons

baskets are the main containers for dry goods

potter's workshop

olive press

ceramic jars are filled with wine or oil and thrown away when they are empty

the potter shapes his jars in the "Pompeii" pattern

hurdles (willow fences)

The house prospers
150 B.C.

Not everyone in Pompeii lives in a big house. As the city grows, poorer families rent tiny apartments in *cenacula* (apartment blocks). The stores below open out onto the street. Cheaply built, the apartment blocks are crumbling.

The house on the opposite side of the street is now very fashionable. The wealthy owner has added a small garden. Decorators are painting the columns that hold up the tiled roof surrounding it. Called a peristyle, the garden is a cool, peaceful haven from the bustle of the street outside.

In the front of the house is a seafood bar. A freed slave (a freedman) runs it, renting his store from his former owner. Customers choose their food from the warmed jars that are set into the marble counter. Visitors to the town are not the only customers. Many of the apartments opposite do not have kitchens, so their tenants buy food "to go."

families share tiny rooms in an apartment building

getting rid of dirt and dust

stores

foreign traders from Pompeii's docks

snack bar

In crowded apartments the kitchen, dining room, bedroom, and bathroom are all in the same room.

badly built apartments are in danger of collapsing

stone blocks in the road are shaped to fit tightly together

wealthy houses with lavish peristyle gardens

Hungry street children steal food from the open counters of the snack bar.

people drive carts on the right-hand side of the road

peristyle (courtyard garden)

walls and columns are painted to look like expensive marble

slaves tend the shrubs

garbage and dirt will be swept away by the rain

once a farmhouse, this building is now a fashionable town house

the owner greets visitors in the tablinum (office)

atrium (paved courtyard)

seafood bar

freedman owner of the bar

fresh fish cooked to order

visitors buy snacks, and local people buy food to eat at home

13

Inside the atrium
100 B.C.

Every grand house in Pompeii has an atrium—a paved courtyard. Its roof drains rainwater into a central pool. The pool overflows into a buried cistern (tank), which supplies drinking water. The atrium is not only a way to collect water, it also cools the surrounding rooms. The atrium's size and decorations show off the owner's wealth.

fake windows are painted on the walls

the peristyle can be seen from the atrium

the house owner greets a visitor

the atrium is a less private area where official callers can wait to see the house owner

a slave attends to the waiting clients

tablinum (office)

pet bird

access hole leading to the cistern

rainwater falls into the impluvium (pool) to keep the atrium cool and then overflows into a cistern below, to be collected as drinking water

Drawing water from the cistern is easier than using the deep wells in town.

expensive mosaic floor

The shady atrium is the center of life in the house. Children play on the cool tiles around the shallow pool. Slaves come to collect water. The master of the house greets visitors in the tablinum, a room that overlooks the atrium. The overhanging roof of the atrium means that this "outdoor room" is comfortable, even during the rare summer storms.

In a side room a Greek slave teaches the children. They learn reading and writing by chanting poems and copying letters onto wax-coated boards. Misbehaving children are hit with canes across the hand or whipped over the back. The teacher reminds them of what the Greek thinker Aristotle once said . . . "all learning is painful."

the walls are painted to look like expensive marble

thick double doors close off the school room from the noisy atrium

Poorer children are taught by fellow Pompeii citizens in outdoor "street schools."

archways show off the entire house to the people looking in from the street

children play with dolls, balls, and wooden toy animals

a Greek slave serves as a pedagogus (teacher) for wealthy boys at home

the blunt end of the stylus (writing tool) erases errors in the wax-coated writing board

15

The city under attack
89 B.C.

An urgent message echoes through the streets . . .
"The Romans are at the gates!" As soon as this news
reaches the house, giant catapults start to pound the roofs
with rocks. The people of Pompeii are fighting against
Roman rule and demanding equal treatment to
Roman people. The Romans have sent their army
to show that they still control Italy.

fights break out in every street between Roman soldiers and Pompeii's rebels

the house suffers terrible damage

Springs made from animal gristle power the Roman ballista (stone hurler).

seafood bar

fires spread from the damaged bakery

stepping stones

thermopolium (hot food bar)

citizens escaping from danger

cart carrying weapons and supplies for the Roman army

Roman soldiers march in

The attack terrifies the family in the
house, but it also angers them. They do not
want to be second-class citizens. So, like people
in other Italian towns, they are fighting against the
mighty Roman army. They were ready for the attack
and have stored weapons to fight back, but they know
that they have little chance of winning the battle.

the ballista fires grapefruit-sized rocks, which can cause a lot of damage

clay tiles shatter easily

rocks batter down walls and roofs, forcing people to flee from their houses

Pompeii's rebels paint directions on the walls for those defending the city.

fleeing citizens

rebels fight back

The Roman army is well trained, with the best weapons and equipment. They soon surround Pompeii and demand that the citizens surrender. Their catapults smash buildings; flaming missiles start fires. As the city walls crumble, the rebellion does too. Columns of soldiers march through the streets. Pompeii is defeated! Fearing revenge attacks, the family abandons the house.

After the war
82 B.C.

Pompeii's people are punished for their rebellion. After the war, their Roman rulers make the town a colony—a settlement for retired soldiers. One of these soldiers takes over the house. He rebuilds its shattered roof and knocks down some walls. He uses the abandoned building next door as a stable.

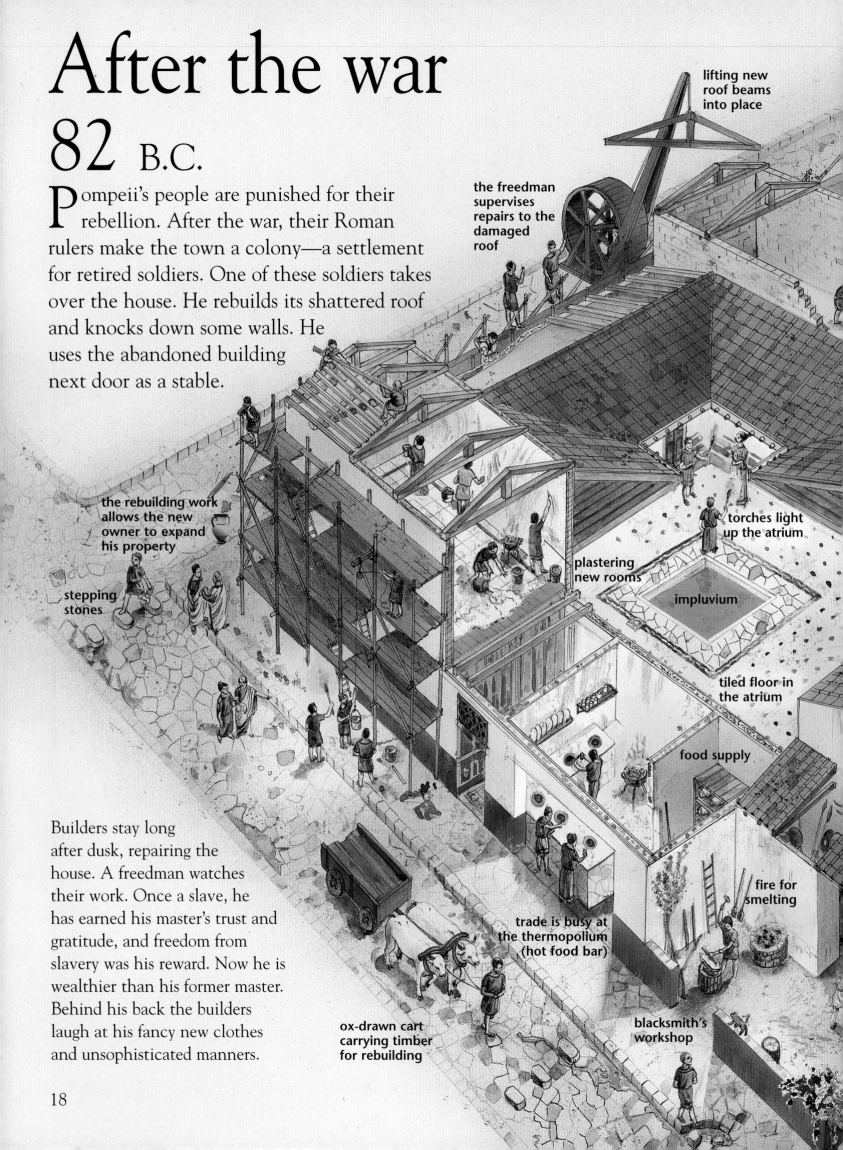

lifting new roof beams into place

the freedman supervises repairs to the damaged roof

the rebuilding work allows the new owner to expand his property

stepping stones

torches light up the atrium

plastering new rooms

impluvium

tiled floor in the atrium

food supply

fire for smelting

trade is busy at the thermopolium (hot food bar)

ox-drawn cart carrying timber for rebuilding

blacksmith's workshop

Builders stay long after dusk, repairing the house. A freedman watches their work. Once a slave, he has earned his master's trust and gratitude, and freedom from slavery was his reward. Now he is wealthier than his former master. Behind his back the builders laugh at his fancy new clothes and unsophisticated manners.

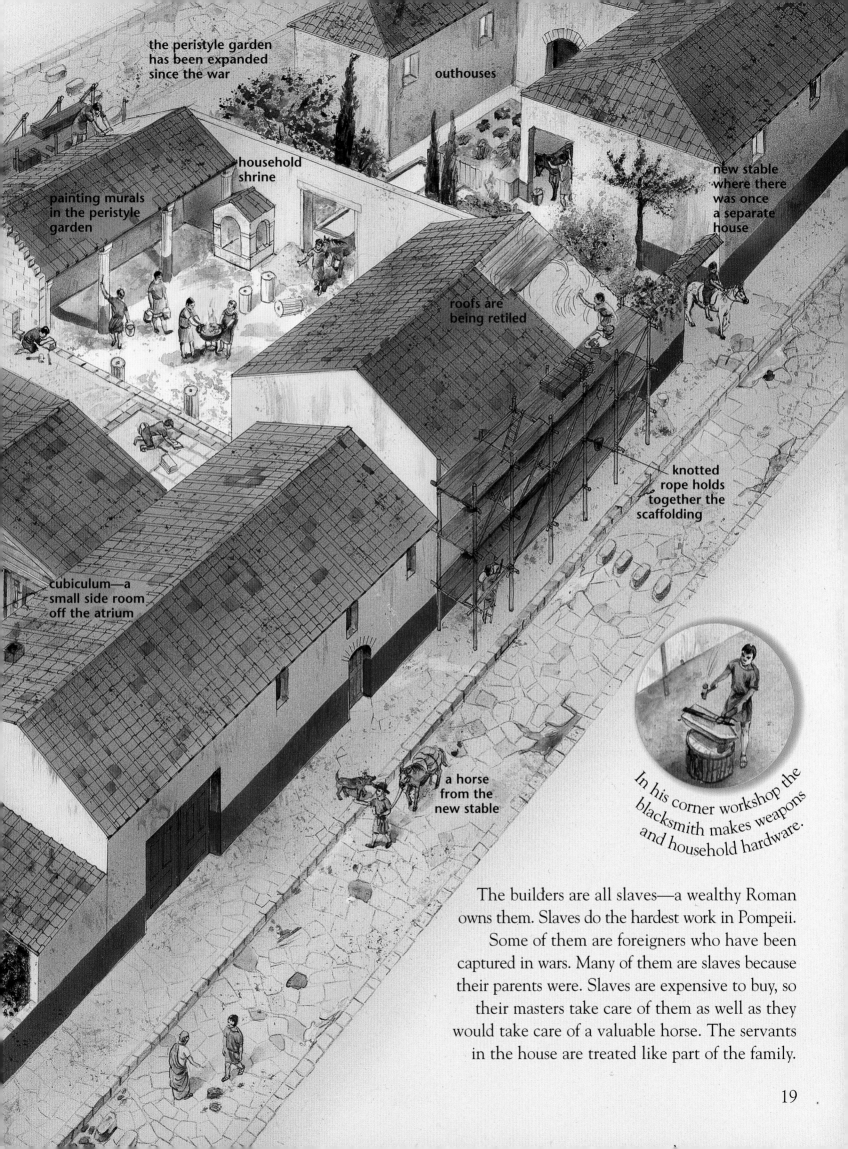

the peristyle garden has been expanded since the war

household shrine

outhouses

new stable where there was once a separate house

painting murals in the peristyle garden

roofs are being retiled

knotted rope holds together the scaffolding

cubiculum—a small side room off the atrium

a horse from the new stable

In his corner workshop the blacksmith makes weapons and household hardware.

The builders are all slaves—a wealthy Roman owns them. Slaves do the hardest work in Pompeii. Some of them are foreigners who have been captured in wars. Many of them are slaves because their parents were. Slaves are expensive to buy, so their masters take care of them as well as they would take care of a valuable horse. The servants in the house are treated like part of the family.

19

A growing city
A.D. 10

Ninety-two years later the quiet street outside of the house has grown into a busy highway. The ox-drawn carts, donkeys, and people moving along the road are all heading for the forum. At the western end of Pompeii the forum is in the most important part of the city. Around this grand square there are markets, government offices, temples, and baths.

The forum shows just how Roman Pompeii has become. All around you can see the Latin language of the Roman colonists who settled there after the war. Latin is on food and fabric stalls, on government notices, and even in the graffiti scrawled on the lavatory walls. The Romans also brought their religion with them, adding new temples dedicated to their gods and goddesses.

a horse and chariot speeding along a quiet street

Warm-air heating, called a hypocaust, keeps the floor and water warm in the forum baths.

street trader's stall selling foreign goods

grain market

street traders

a one-way traffic system is now operating in the city to prevent too many accidents

wealthy houses with large, lavish peristyle gardens

bakery

Temple of Apollo

Stretched canvas shades the audience in the outdoor theater.

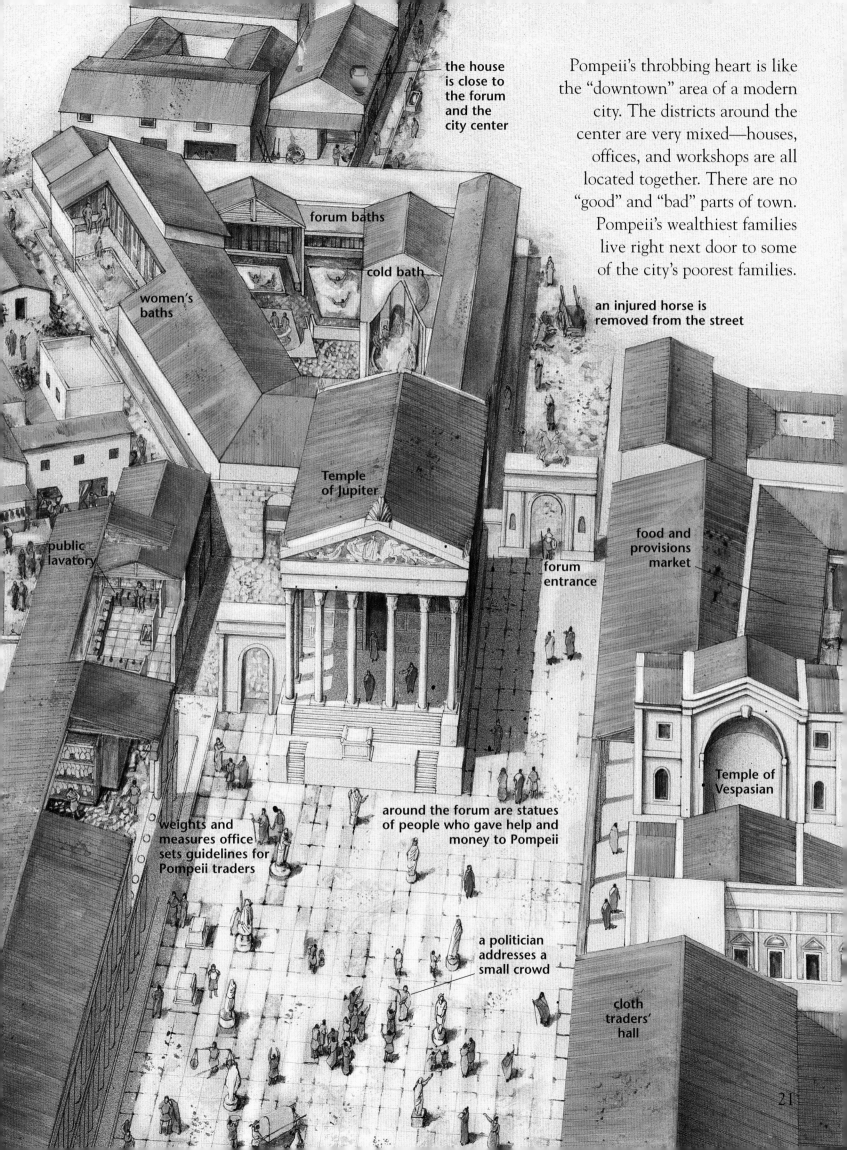

the house is close to the forum and the city center

forum baths

cold bath

women's baths

Pompeii's throbbing heart is like the "downtown" area of a modern city. The districts around the center are very mixed—houses, offices, and workshops are all located together. There are no "good" and "bad" parts of town. Pompeii's wealthiest families live right next door to some of the city's poorest families.

an injured horse is removed from the street

Temple of Jupiter

food and provisions market

forum entrance

public lavatory

Temple of Vespasian

weights and measures office sets guidelines for Pompeii traders

around the forum are statues of people who gave help and money to Pompeii

a politician addresses a small crowd

cloth traders' hall

21

The house at its peak
A.D. 60

Glittering with marble mosaics and echoing with the splash of cooling fountains, the house has become luxurious, calm, and comfortable. From the street door, visitors look through enchanting open spaces and rooms into distant gardens. The wealthy family living there has made the house magnificent. Within its walls they feel safe from harm.

Water has helped make the house even grander than before. Since an aqueduct (water channel) reached Pompeii, rich families have had water piped into their homes. The water spouts out from fountains and keeps the gardens green, even in the dry heat of the summer.

Water towers distribute the water that is carried to Pompeii by the aqueduct.

Despite these water supplies, Pompeii's streets smell bad. Most people empty sewage into the gutter, relying on storms to wash it away. Until it rains, high curbs and stepping stones keep people's feet high up and away from the dirt.

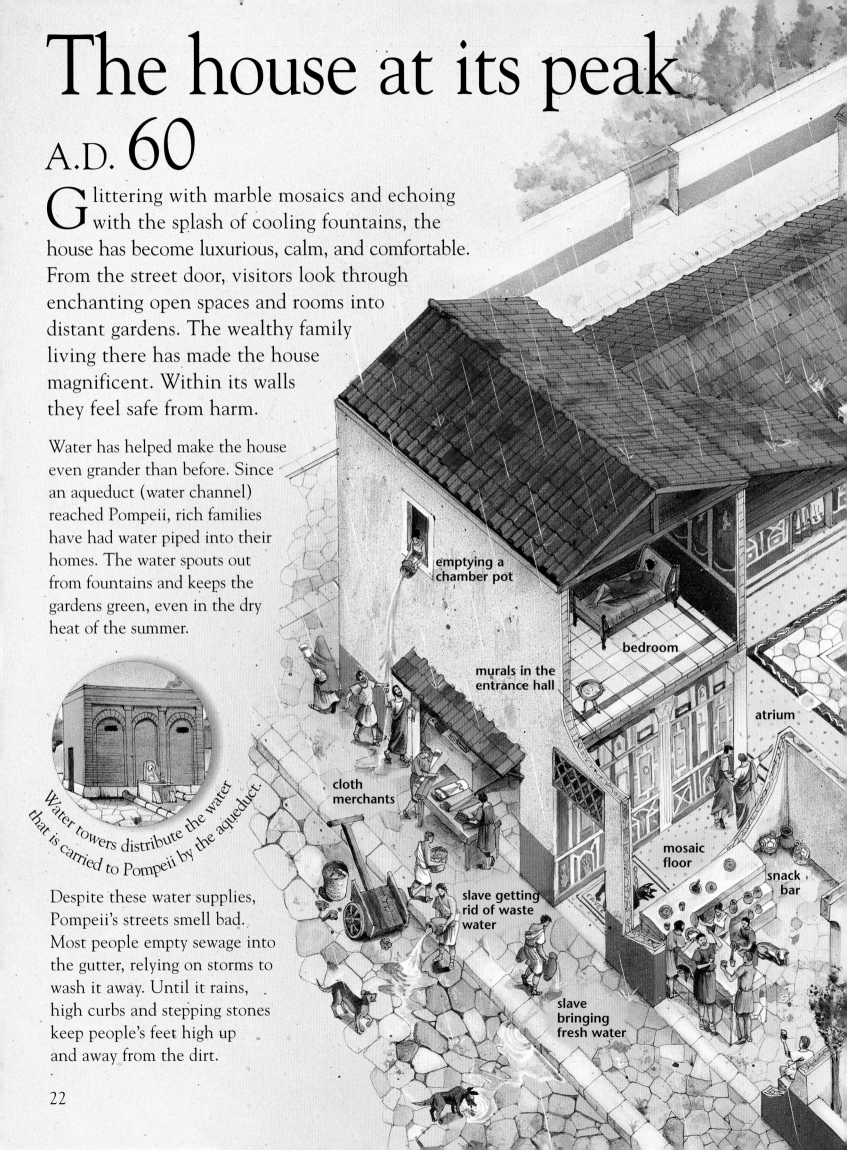

emptying a chamber pot

murals in the entrance hall

bedroom

atrium

cloth merchants

mosaic floor

snack bar

slave getting rid of waste water

slave bringing fresh water

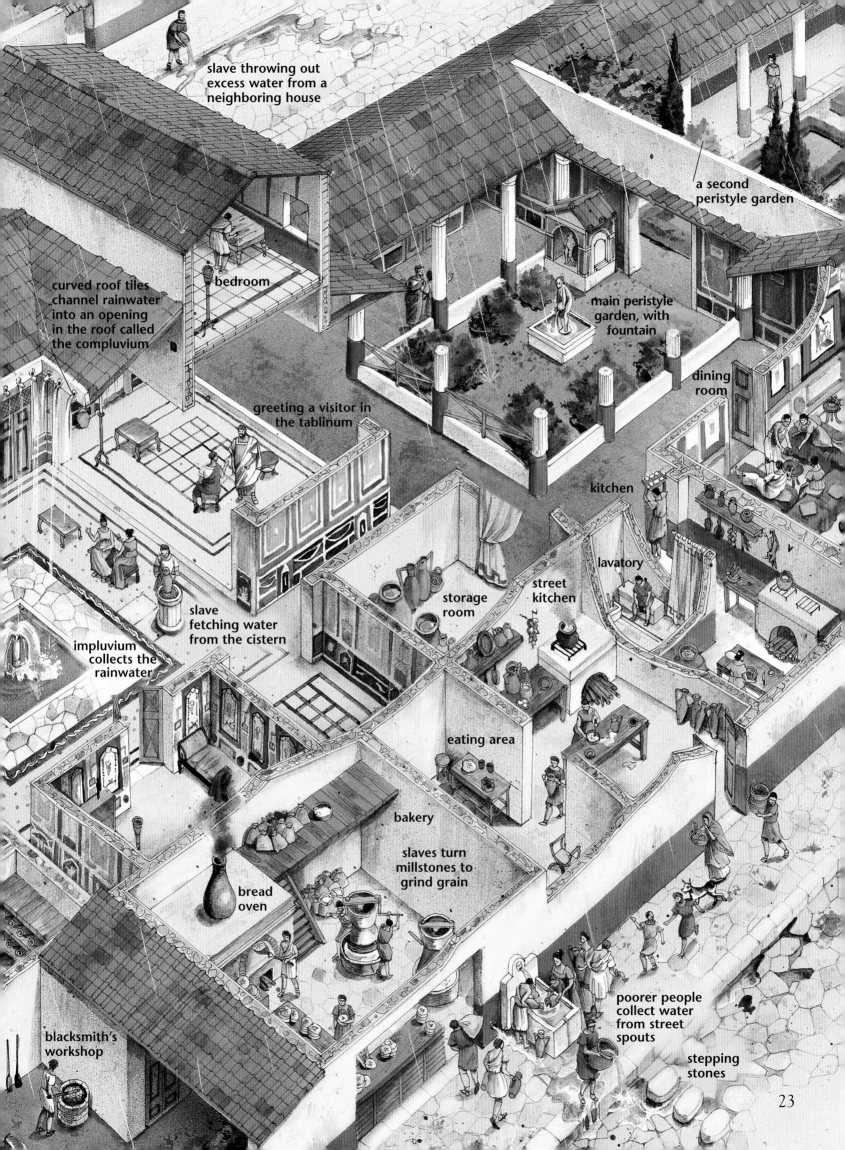

slave throwing out excess water from a neighboring house

a second peristyle garden

curved roof tiles channel rainwater into an opening in the roof called the compluvium

bedroom

main peristyle garden, with fountain

greeting a visitor in the tablinum

dining room

kitchen

slave fetching water from the cistern

lavatory

impluvium collects the rainwater

street kitchen

storage room

eating area

bakery

bread oven

slaves turn millstones to grind grain

blacksmith's workshop

poorer people collect water from street spouts

stepping stones

the peristyle garden is a private space for friends and family

slaves tend the garden and pick flowers for the banquet

slaves bringing more food

jar of garum—an expensive cooking sauce made from rotten fish guts

lavatory

plucking poultry

a second kitchen serves the outdoor snack bar

A banquet
A.D. 60

As the sun sets, the sound of music and laughter disturbs the quiet street. There is a banquet in the house, in honor of an important politician. Free-flowing wine has made the guests very relaxed. They lounge on the three gently sloping couches in the triclinium (dining room). The meal is almost finished.

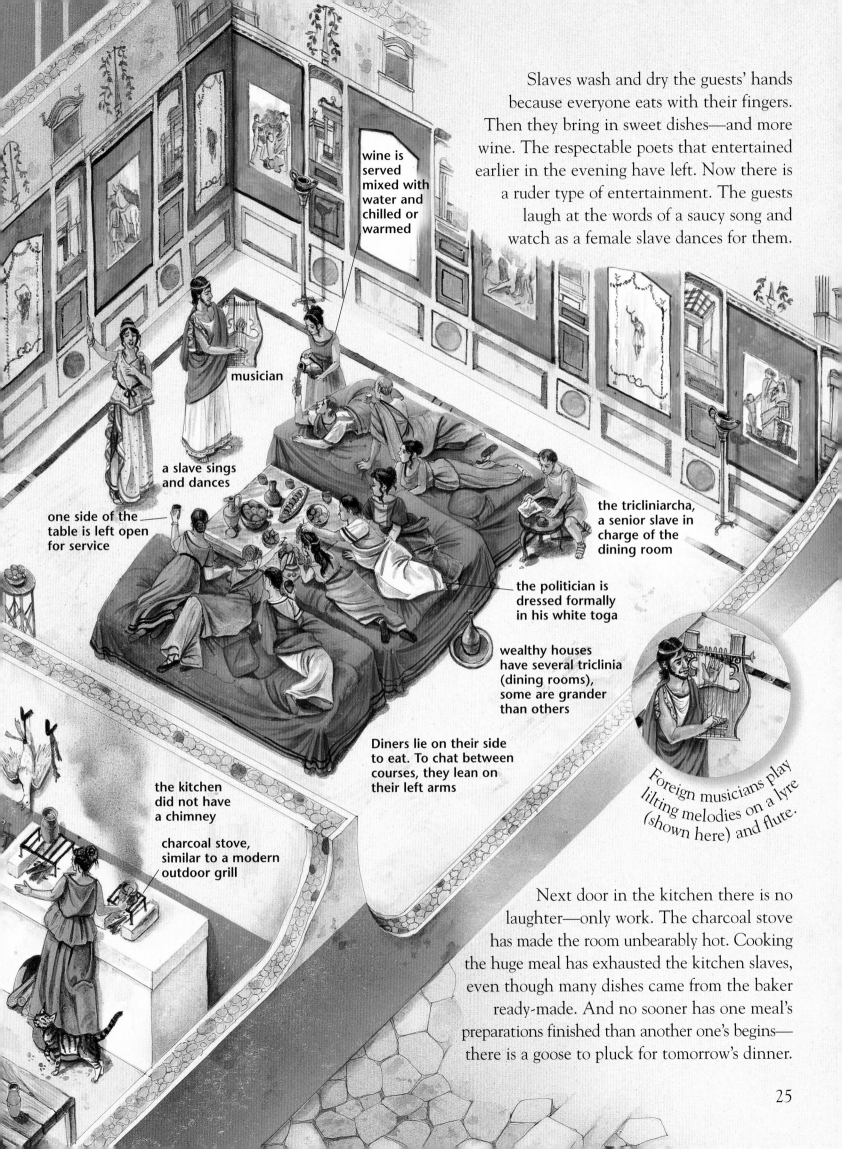

Slaves wash and dry the guests' hands because everyone eats with their fingers. Then they bring in sweet dishes—and more wine. The respectable poets that entertained earlier in the evening have left. Now there is a ruder type of entertainment. The guests laugh at the words of a saucy song and watch as a female slave dances for them.

wine is served mixed with water and chilled or warmed

musician

a slave sings and dances

one side of the table is left open for service

the tricliniarcha, a senior slave in charge of the dining room

the politician is dressed formally in his white toga

wealthy houses have several triclinia (dining rooms), some are grander than others

Diners lie on their side to eat. To chat between courses, they lean on their left arms

Foreign musicians play lilting melodies on a lyre (shown here) and flute.

the kitchen did not have a chimney

charcoal stove, similar to a modern outdoor grill

Next door in the kitchen there is no laughter—only work. The charcoal stove has made the room unbearably hot. Cooking the huge meal has exhausted the kitchen slaves, even though many dishes came from the baker ready-made. And no sooner has one meal's preparations finished than another one's begins—there is a goose to pluck for tomorrow's dinner.

The earthquake
A.D. 62

It starts as a tremor—just enough to rattle the plates in the kitchen and send a ripple across the pools. Nobody is worried. The people of Pompeii are used to earthquakes. Sometimes they crack a wall or two; few do any real harm. And it is February—there has never been a bad earthquake in the winter. Until now . . .

When the earthquake strikes, it feels as if the fire god, Vulcan, has picked up the house and shaken it. The atrium columns sway. Mosaic floors buck like angry horses. Everybody falls to the ground. This is just the beginning. Amid a terrifying roar, a giant crack opens up in the road outside. A dog tumbles into it.

After the earthquake, people return to their houses to rescue those people who were trapped in the rubble.

Then, as quickly as it appeared, the crack closes up. The walls of the triclinium teeter and fall down; other walls are split with several cracks. Red clay tiles slide off the roof and shatter on the ground. Water stops flowing from the fountains. Instead, it gushes out of holes in the road—at least, it does until the aqueduct runs dry.

the badly built apartments suffer the worst damage

fires start where the earthquake has overturned cooking stoves

trees fall down

weak walls collapse

a slave salvages his belongings and heads for safety

a foreign trader flees to the harbor

an escaped guard dog chases the citizens

children are carried away from danger

birds fly out of the quivering trees

rooms around the peristyle are destroyed

balconies collapse and fall into the street below

people run from damaged buildings

falling tiles injure people in the streets

rubble buries slaves trapped inside of the houses

thieves take advantage of the chaos

the walls and roofs of the house suffer the most damage

deep cracks open up in Pompeii's streets

cracks open up, even in the sturdiest walls

a frightened horse bolts

water floods out from damaged pipes

people are rescued from collapsing buildings

27.

After the earthquake A.D. 70

Eight years after the earthquake Pompeii still has not returned to normal. There are cracked walls and collapsed buildings on every street. The lives of some of Pompeii's people will never be the same again. Some people left the city for good, terrified of another tremor. The poorer people stayed—where else could they go? And for some people the earthquake was a golden opportunity.

The earthquake did not destroy every building in the city, but many were so badly damaged that their owners could not afford to repair them. Wealthy next-door neighbors snapped up the abandoned homes. So the house at the crossroads is now even bigger and grander.

Builders have become wealthy. With everyone desperate for repairs, builders are able to double their fees. For cheaper houses they make rushed repairs to cover the worst of the damage. But Pompeii's rich want their homes rebuilt more lavishly than they were before. There is even a new fashion in decoration. Now artists paint blank walls to look like windows and doors with views out onto fantastic landscapes.

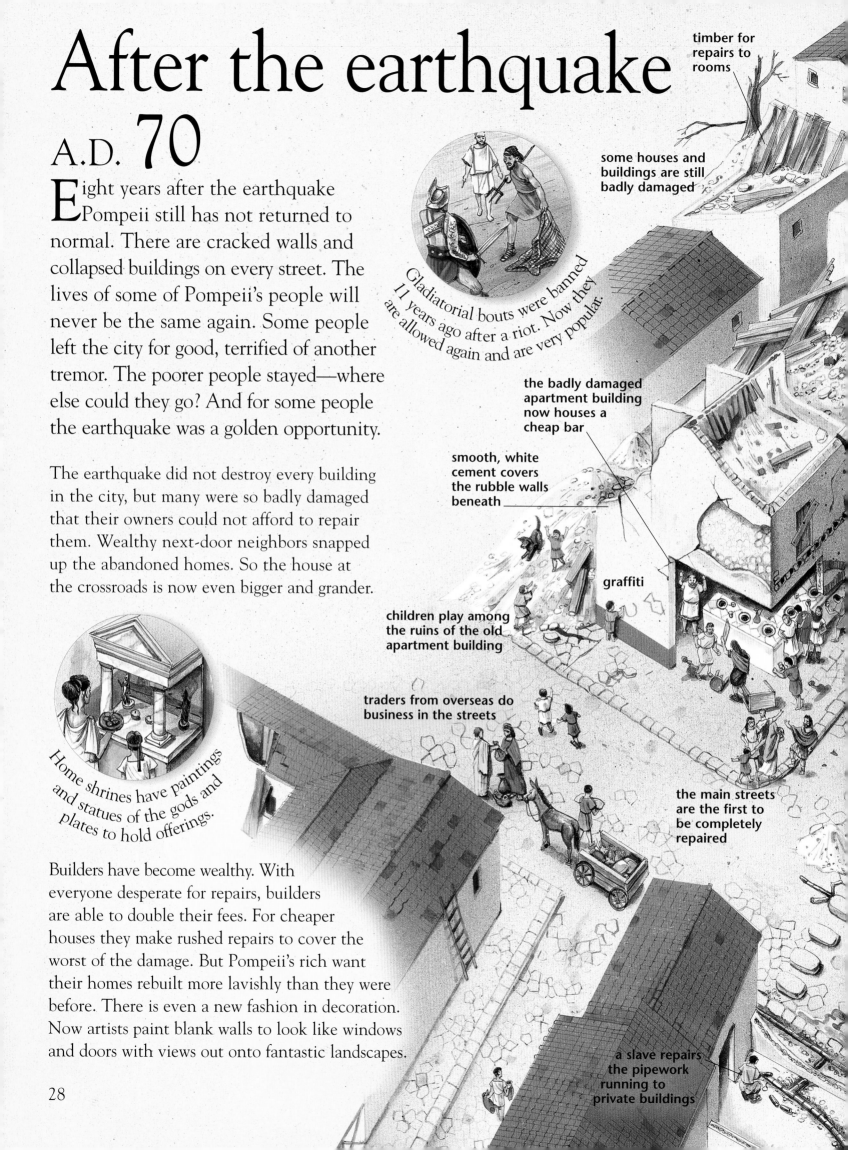

timber for repairs to rooms

some houses and buildings are still badly damaged

Gladiatorial bouts were banned 11 years ago after a riot. Now they are allowed again and are very popular.

the badly damaged apartment building now houses a cheap bar

smooth, white cement covers the rubble walls beneath

graffiti

children play among the ruins of the old apartment building

Home shrines have paintings and statues of the gods and plates to hold offerings.

traders from overseas do business in the streets

the main streets are the first to be completely repaired

a slave repairs the pipework running to private buildings

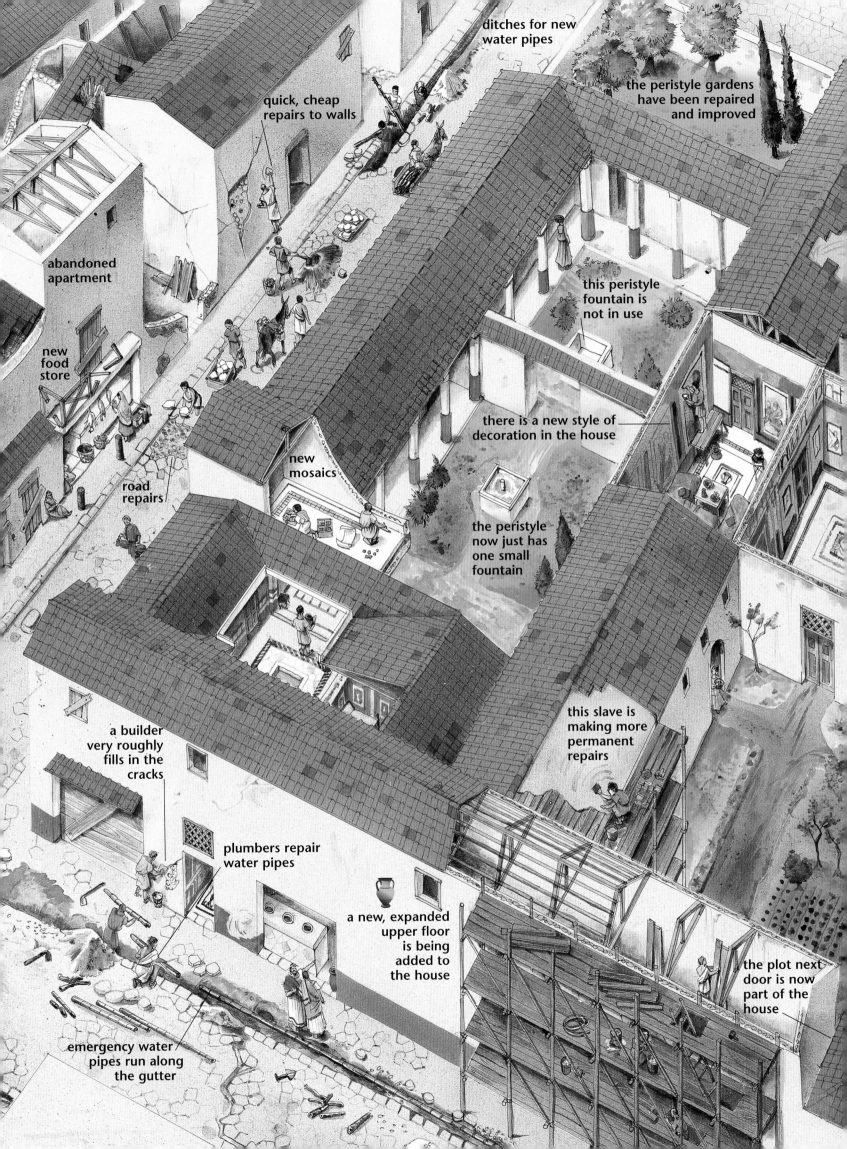

ditches for new water pipes

quick, cheap repairs to walls

the peristyle gardens have been repaired and improved

abandoned apartment

this peristyle fountain is not in use

new food store

there is a new style of decoration in the house

road repairs

new mosaics

the peristyle now just has one small fountain

a builder very roughly fills in the cracks

this slave is making more permanent repairs

plumbers repair water pipes

a new, expanded upper floor is being added to the house

the plot next door is now part of the house

emergency water pipes run along the gutter

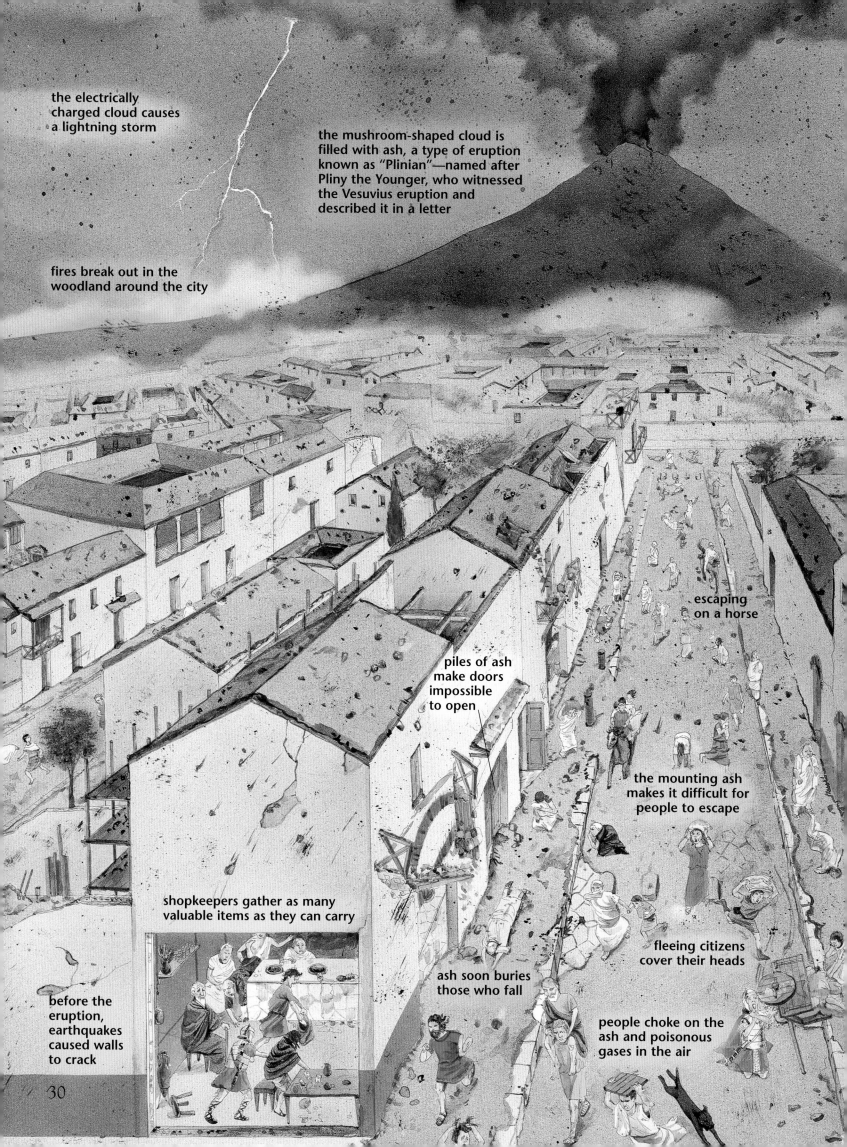

the electrically charged cloud causes a lightning storm

the mushroom-shaped cloud is filled with ash, a type of eruption known as "Plinian"—named after Pliny the Younger, who witnessed the Vesuvius eruption and described it in a letter

fires break out in the woodland around the city

escaping on a horse

piles of ash make doors impossible to open

the mounting ash makes it difficult for people to escape

shopkeepers gather as many valuable items as they can carry

fleeing citizens cover their heads

ash soon buries those who fall

before the eruption, earthquakes caused walls to crack

people choke on the ash and poisonous gases in the air

The eruption

A.D. 79

S mall, strange things make the morning of August 24, A.D. 79 different from other mornings. Wells dry up. Dogs howl. All of the birds stop singing. There are tremors in the ground. At the time nobody thinks about these things as warning signs. After all, tremors are not unusual during the summer in Pompeii. But then, during the hottest part of the day, it happens. With an awful, deafening roar, Vesuvius explodes.

People use pillows and baskets to protect themselves from the falling cinders and lumps of lava.

the falling ash turns into hot cinders, causing fires to break out

ash and pumice form a thick layer on roofs

a roof collapses under the weight of the ash and pumice

The eruption blasts the top part of the mountain high up into the sky, blotting out the sun. Half an hour later ash begins to fall on Pompeii like hot, black snow. In two hours it is knee-deep. The terrified population flees, grabbing whatever they can carry. By dusk most people have left Pompeii.

Most . . . but not all. The rich owner of the house at the crossroads stays inside, fearing looters will rob him. Other people take cover inside of the closest building, hoping that they will be safe. Shopkeepers who return to collect their gold delay their escape for too long. By dawn they are all dead, killed by falling roofs, poisonous gas from the mountain, or the fiery cloud that rolls over the city.

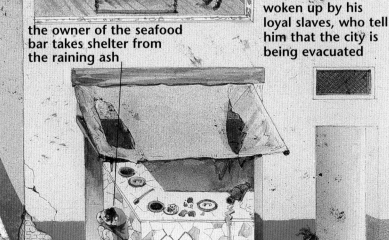

the house owner is woken up by his loyal slaves, who tell him that the city is being evacuated

the owner of the seafood bar takes shelter from the raining ash

a dog chokes and struggles above the rising ash

A buried city
A.D. 100

Where a bustling, glittering city once stood, now there is only a desert of ash. A river and the sea once lapped at Pompeii's walls, but not anymore. The eruption changed the coast and rerouted the river. The nearby town of Herculaneum is buried even deeper than Pompeii. The disaster alarms all of the Roman people. Even the emperor, Titus, comes to inspect the damage.

Titus can do little more than watch as Pompeii's people try to salvage what they can from the ruins. They can barely see the outline of the buried city's streets. Some people make tunnels to recover the precious possessions that they left behind or to find bronze statues from the forum. Soon the city becomes a quarry, as builders dig up marble and even paving stones.

Some of their discoveries are not as welcome. Soon after the eruption, the ash hardened around those people who did not escape in time. Now their corpses have rotted into skeletons. The salvage workers find the bones inside of body-shaped hollows at the bottom of the ash. They shudder and offer a quick prayer to Vulcan, the Roman god of fire.

The eruption has greatly enlarged the crater of Vesuvius, and the mighty volcano is at rest once again.

digging through to buried buildings in the forum

new vegetation sprouts out of the soil, which is very fertile because of all the ash from the eruption

Larger tunnels are dug to reach parts of the forum area in order to find valuable public items such as statues.

Valuable items are recovered from the forum and returned to Rome as part of the official salvage operation.

the tunnels are filled in once items have been salvaged

statues and other valuable items are found and removed

the top part of a temple in the forum has been uncovered

the top of a tower sticks up through the ash and is raided for building materials

The lower part of the house is still buried under several feet of volcanic ash.

digging has exposed the remains of the upper story of the house

this doorway shows where the main entrance into the atrium once was

workers dig down to uncover buried buildings

a farmer plants new vines

a worker collects paving stones

only the tops of walls are visible after the digging

workers remove stone and materials to be used in new buildings

Forgotten Pompeii
A.D. 1689

Sixteen hundred years have passed since Vesuvius erupted so violently. The local people now call the neighborhood "la Città" (the city)—they do not even remember Pompeii's name. The farmers who grow apricots and vines on the rich, black soil never suspect that the roots of their crops curl around beautiful statues in the peristylium of the house at the crossroads.

However . . . from time to time Pompeii reveals a handful of its secrets, reminding Italians of the lost civilization that is buried beneath their feet. Around 1600, laborers digging a canal cut through the lower floors of Pompeii's buildings. But nobody pays much attention to the coins that they find or to the letters carved on the stones that they dig up.

vineyard

the volcanic soil is rich in minerals and ideal for agriculture

wine press

the farm owner

the farmers keep horses for pulling carts and plows

rain soaks quickly into the light soil, so the crops and vines will need extra water from the new well

the soil is light and easy to till by hand

the local residents no longer fear the volcano's power

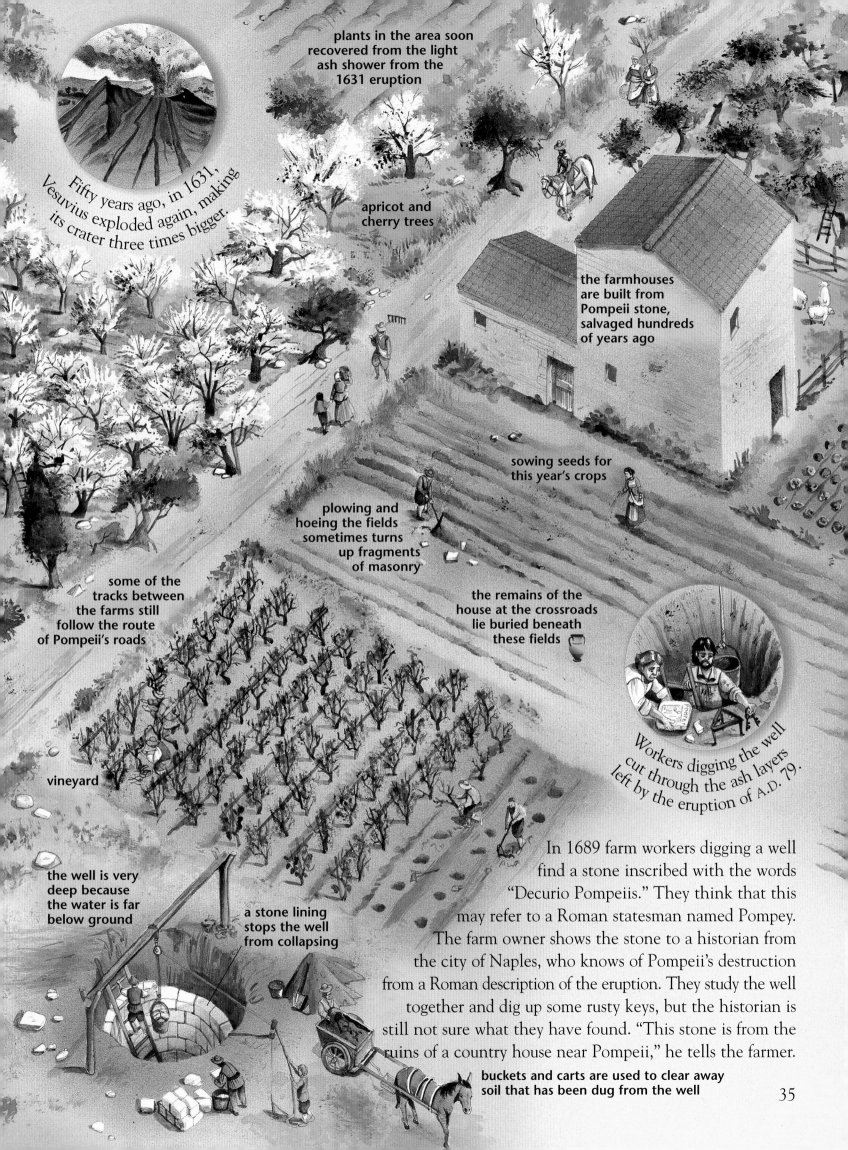

Fifty years ago, in 1631, Vesuvius exploded again, making its crater three times bigger.

plants in the area soon recovered from the light ash shower from the 1631 eruption

apricot and cherry trees

the farmhouses are built from Pompeii stone, salvaged hundreds of years ago

sowing seeds for this year's crops

plowing and hoeing the fields sometimes turns up fragments of masonry

some of the tracks between the farms still follow the route of Pompeii's roads

the remains of the house at the crossroads lie buried beneath these fields

Workers digging the well cut through the ash layers left by the eruption of A.D. 79

vineyard

the well is very deep because the water is far below ground

a stone lining stops the well from collapsing

In 1689 farm workers digging a well find a stone inscribed with the words "Decurio Pompeiis." They think that this may refer to a Roman statesman named Pompey. The farm owner shows the stone to a historian from the city of Naples, who knows of Pompeii's destruction from a Roman description of the eruption. They study the well together and dig up some rusty keys, but the historian is still not sure what they have found. "This stone is from the ruins of a country house near Pompeii," he tells the farmer.

buckets and carts are used to clear away soil that has been dug from the well

35

before scientific archaeology begins in the 1800s, all excavations are like those taking place in Pompeii

these scholars are not interested in the pattern of Pompeii's walls—they are simply looking for precious items

wooden panels prevent the soil from falling in while a ruin is being explored

groups of prison convicts are forced to help with the digging

Pompeii's famous wall paintings, inside, suddenly make Roman-style decoration very fashionable in Europe

wealthy Europeans visit to watch excavators stage "discoveries" of precious objects reburied earlier

Treasure hunters A.D. 1750

In the spring of 1748 Giacopo Martorelli is certain that he will discover Pompeii: "It lies beneath la Cività!," he tells anyone who will listen. Martorelli, a professor of Greek literature, is a very persuasive man. Digging begins in April, and success comes quickly: the workers discover beautiful wall paintings, a Roman helmet, oil lamps, and coins.

An inscription on a stone, found in 1763, proves beyond a doubt that la Città lies on the site of Pompeii.

Within three weeks the first skeleton is found, along with a handful of gold and silver. This small heap of money encourages a hunt for more, and frantic digging begins. The search for Pompeii turns into a treasure hunt.

In the years that follow some amazing finds are made. Shovels strike sparks from the stones, as workers uncover the house at the crossroads. But, for the scholars in charge, valuable ornaments are what matter. Whenever they stop finding beautiful paintings and gold or silver statues, they simply fill in the holes and move on.

Carelessness, rivalry, and greed scatter Pompeii's riches. The king of Naples takes the best of the art for his private collection. The less impressive pieces are deliberately smashed so that they cannot be sold illegally. Criminals shoveling ash, as part of their punishment, pocket small treasures. And nobody bothers to keep a record of what they find or where it lies.

two workers fill in a ruin after removing its treasures

ash has preserved the seafood bar attached to the house

the position of these ruins is not recorded—later in the 1700s more detailed plans of the finds are made

wheelbarrows are used to move the ash away and dump it nearby

Scholars are allowed to study the finds, but only if they have been specially invited by the king.

the Pompeii diggings become a popular attraction for foreigners, starting a brief fashion for Roman-style decoration all over Europe

Fiorelli's excavations connect previously uncovered areas

workers use brushes and trowels to remove the ash carefully

Fiorelli had been imprisoned for his part in the Italian revolution

a worker mixes some plaster of Paris for casting

the archaeologists also use plaster casting to make imitations of wooden objects such as doors

once the plaster casts have set, they are carefully dug out of the ground

the methods that Fiorelli teaches will soon be in use on all digs

Studying the ruins
A.D. 1870

Removing Pompeii's artifacts, without describing where they were found, is disastrous. It robs Italians of their history. The excavations are recorded better in the 1800s, but scientific study only begins in 1861, after a revolution unites Italy's many kingdoms into a single country. The king of this new country is Vittorio Emanuele (1820–1878).

The archaeologists use liquid plaster of Paris to make casts of the corpses. It hardens in minutes.

Fiorelli gives each region, street block, and door an "address" to help with the recording of finds in these areas

skeletons are found in and around the house and the seafood bar

the body casts show where people fell as they tried to escape or protect themselves

this cast is of a dog that died outside of the seafood bar

soil and ash are taken off the site in wheelbarrows and carts

the archaeologists work on one street block at a time

the plaster peels off where the flesh is thin, revealing skulls and kneecaps

an archaeologist makes a written note of where this body was found and in what position

The king of Italy puts the archaeologist Giuseppe Fiorelli (1823–1896) in charge of Pompeii. Fiorelli has exciting new ideas. Under his guidance, experts remove the ash from every room in the house at the crossroads, instead of digging small holes. They make a note of everything that they find, however worthless it seems at the time. Fiorelli is a pioneer of stratigraphy—the simple but excellent idea that the oldest objects are buried the deepest in the ground.

The casts of Pompeii's dead, displayed in Fiorelli's museum, fill visitors with sorrow and pity.

Fiorelli also believes that his job is not to find treasure, but to build up a picture of the lives of the people of Pompeii. But it is not life but death that makes Fiorelli famous. He notices that Pompeii's skeletons lie inside of hollows in the ash. He realizes that the hollows trace the shapes of their rotted bodies. Fiorelli fills the hollows with plaster. Removing the surrounding ash creates realistic casts of the people of Pompeii at the moment that Vesuvius smothered them.

Romantic ruins *Today*

The grand house in Pompeii echoes with voices once again. Each day around 7,000 people visit the city. They gaze in wonder at the cobbled roads, preserved houses, and colorful mosaic decorations. They stare silently at the casts of the city's dead, and tour guides retell Pompeii's tragic story—which has not ended yet.

Pompeii is dying once again. The city is huge, and Italy's archaeologists do not have enough money to protect it all. In the house at the crossroads weather destroys the murals. Walls collapse where weeds and trees dislodge the masonry. Vandals carve their names in the stone and steal souvenirs.

But the news is not all bad. Tourists buy tickets to visit Pompeii's ruins, and in 1997 a law was passed to ensure that the money from ticket sales is spent on improving and maintaining the site. New conservation projects are being developed to preserve the ruins while also exploring areas that are still uncovered. So one day we may have an even better picture of the city where life suddenly stopped almost 2,000 years ago.

the apartment block is easy to recognize by the many doorways leading up from street level

children play on the stepping stones

cheap food bar

the cobbled streets punish those foolish enough to wear high-heeled shoes

Digging up a single fish scale can help archaeologists figure out what Pompeii's people ate.

stray dogs roam Pompeii's streets—just as they did before the eruption

archaeologists find big mutton bones in this cheap bar and the small bones of lamb in the expensive house opposite

peristyle garden

peristyle garden

wooden scaffolding reinforces weak walls and keeps visitors at a safe distance

marble-effect paint has peeled, showing the cheap brick that it covered

tablinum

the peristyle gardens have been planted with flowers and trees again

atrium

sections of the house and seafood bar have been partially restored to show how they once looked

ruts worn by carts' wheels show which way the traffic flowed

tourists visiting the house at the crossroads learn about its history from a tour guide

The perfectly preserved forum baths are the first stop for many of Pompeii's tourists.

VI VIII

Glossary

Words in *italics* refer to other glossary entries.

aqueduct
A trough, bridge, or pipe carrying drinking water from a water source to towns and cities.

archaeologist
A scientist who studies *archaeology*.

archaeology
Learning about how people lived in the past by studying what remains of them and the things that they built and made.

artifacts
Handmade objects, often found in archaeological *excavations*.

atrium
A courtyard in a house with a surrounding roof that drains rainwater into a central pool or *impluvium*.

ballista
A giant *catapult* that hurls rocks to batter down walls during warfare.

baths
A public place for washing and relaxation, similar to today's spas.

blacksmith
Someone who heats and hammers iron to shape it into useful things.

casting
Pouring a liquid into a hollow so that when the liquid hardens, it copies the shape of the hollow.

catapult
A weapon that uses spring power to hurl rocks or stones at an enemy.

cenacula
Blocks of apartments or an apartment building.

chariot
A fast, two-wheeled horse-drawn war cart that carries soldiers.

cistern
A large tank for storing drinking water.

(la) Città
"The City"—the name used for the region where Pompeii once stood until the city was uncovered.

Vesuvius lies on the coast of the Bay of Naples, around 6 miles (9km) east of the city of Naples, in southern Italy. The volcano last erupted in 1944.

We do not know for certain how the first residents of Pompeii lived, but elsewhere in Italy they built round, thatched huts, like this one.

colonists
People who set up a place to live in a new land. Sometimes, as in Pompeii, old soldiers were given houses or land as a reward for their services.

compluvium
An open space in the middle of the atrium.

cubiculum
A bedroom.

curb
A row of straight stones at the edge of a road, raised to keep vehicles off the sidewalk.

Emanuele, Vittorio
Italy's first king of modern times. Born in 1820, he ruled from 1861 until his death 17 years later.

emmer
A type of edible grass grown to make flour, until wheat replaced it as a crop.

excavation
An area dug up quickly by treasure hunters or carefully by *archaeologists*, who record and preserve everything that they find.

Fiorelli, Giuseppe
An Italian archaeologist (lived 1823–1896) who introduced scientific methods of excavation in Pompeii from 1861.

forum
The marketplace and central open space of a Roman town.

freedman
A former slave who has been given freedom by his owner.

fresco
A wall painting made by brushing colors onto wet plaster.

fuller
A worker who treats cloth after weaving to clean and thicken it.

fullery
The place where fullers work.

graffiti
Messages scribbled on walls.

gutter
A trough at the side of a road for collecting rainwater and sometimes sewage.

hurdle
A small fence made from thin, bendable sticks that have been woven together.

hypocaust
A furnace-powered heating system that circulates warm air through channels in walls and under floors for private or public *baths*.

Roman hosts thought that nine diners was the perfect number to have around a table.

impluvium
The pool in the middle of an *atrium* for collecting and saving rainwater and for keeping the *atrium* cool.

lararium
The household *shrine* where the family pray to guardian gods and give small offerings.

Latin
The language of the Roman people and the basis for many modern European languages.

lava
The molten rock thrown out by a *volcano*.

livestock
Animals kept by farmers for their meat, milk, wool, or work.

lyre
A small harp played by strumming, like playing a guitar.

marble
A type of very hard, beautiful building stone that can be polished until it is shiny. It was also used in sculptures.

Because of Pompeii's thriving port, the streets were always full of interesting foreign visitors.

Martorelli, Giacopo
A professor of Greek writing in Naples University, who, in the mid-1700s, was among the scholars searching for Pompeii.

masonry
The shaped stones that are used in building.

mosaic
A picture or pattern made up of many pieces of colorful glass, pottery, or stone.

mural
A decorative wall painting.

Naples
A large port on Italy's west coast, overlooking the bay named after it.

pedagogus
A slave who teaches, takes care of, and waits on Roman children.

peristyle garden
A *peristylium* with a garden in the middle.

peristylium
A rectangular courtyard that is supported by columns, with a porch on one or more sides.

plaster of Paris
A white powder that quickly hardens when it is mixed with water.

plaster cast
The reversed copy of an object made by *casting* with *plaster of Paris*.

Plinian eruption
A *volcanic eruption* that throws ash and dust high up into the air, named after the Roman writer who wrote about the eruption of Vesuvius in A.D. 79.

politician
Someone who works in the government and law making, often chosen by the people that they serve.

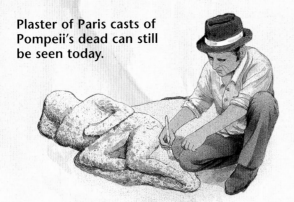

Plaster of Paris casts of Pompeii's dead can still be seen today.

pumice
The foamy rock formed when *lava* sets, often light enough to float in water.

restoration
The repair and improvement of something that has been damaged.

scaffolding
A temporary framework set up next to a wall so that workers standing on it can build or repair.

sewage
The liquid and solid waste from lavatories or from washing.

shrine
A small place for prayer and worship in a *temple*, home, or street.

slave
Someone who is owned and works for their owner and is not free to change their life.

smelting
Heating rock to get out the metal that it contains.

stratigraphy
The science of judging a buried object's age by comparing it with other objects at the same depth in the ground.

stylus
A penlike object that is used to scratch messages.

tablinum
The greeting room in a Roman house between the *atrium* and the *peristylium*.

temple
A place of worship.

tenant
Someone who rents a house or room from the owner of a residence.

thatch
A roofing material made of cut plants such as straw or rushes.

thatched roof
A roof covered in *thatch*.

thermopolium
A bar where food and hot or cold drinks are served.

tourist
Someone who tours a country looking at places of interest—or just someone on vacation.

tricliniarcha
A slave in charge of the *triclinium*.

triclinium
A dining room with three sloping couches, each one big enough for three people, around a table.

Vesuvius
The *volcano* close to Pompeii that erupted in A.D. 79, covering the city in ash.

vineyard
A field where grapevines grow.

volcanic eruption
A violent, often destructive, outflow of *lava*, ash, gas, or other material from a *volcano*.

volcano
A mountain or other place where Earth's liquid core leaks out though gaps in the solid crust.

Vulcan
The Roman god of fire.

The sons of wealthy citizens of Pompeii were taught at home.

45

Index

A tour guide retells the dramatic history of Pompeii.

In the years following the eruption of A.D. 79, Romans visited to salvage precious items and building materials.

Before the eruption that ended life in Pompeii, the city was rocked by an earthquake in A.D. 62.

In the
300s B.C. Pompeii
was already a
thriving center for
trade and agriculture.

KINGFISHER

a Houghton Mifflin Company imprint
222 Berkeley Street
Boston, Massachusetts 02116
www.houghtonmifflinbooks.com

Senior editor: Simon Holland
Coordinating editor: Caitlin Doyle
Senior designer: Heidi Appleton
Cover designer: Jo Connor
Consultant: Dr. Thorsten Opper, Department of Greek
and Roman Antiquities, The British Museum, London, England
Senior production controller: Lindsey Scott
DTP manager: Nicky Studdart
DTP operator: Claire Cessford
Indexer: Carron Brown

First published in 2007
2 4 6 8 10 9 7 5 3 1

1TR/0507/SHENS/CLSN(CLSN)/158MA/C

ISBN: 978-0-7534-6044-3

Copyright © Kingfisher Publications Plc 2007

LIBRARY OF CONGRESS CATALOGING-IN-PUBLICATION DATA
Platt, Richard.
Through time—Pompeii / Richard Platt.
p. cm.
Includes index.
1. Pompeii (Extinct city)—Juvenile literature. 2. Dwellings—Italy—Pompeii (Extinct city)—Juvenile literature.
I. Title.
DG70.P7P58 2007
937'.7—dc22
2007004851

Printed in Taiwan

48